THE ILLUSTRATED
HISTORY OF
AUTOMOBILES

THE ILLUSTRATED HISTORY OF
AUTOMOBILES

David Burgess Wise

Quantum
Books

Title page illustration: 1936 Triumph Dolomite roadster

A QUANTUM BOOK

This book is produced by
Quantum Publishing Ltd.
6 Blundell Street
London N7 9BH

Copyright ©MCMLXXX
Quarto Publishing Limited.

This edition printed 2003

ISBN 1-86160-689-3

QUMIHOA

Printed in Singapore by
Star Standard Industries Pte Ltd.

1936 Auburn 852 supercharged cabriolet

Contents

Introduction

THE MOTOR CAR has been with us now for over a century — little more than the span of a human life — yet it's impossible nowadays to imagine a world without it. Certainly those pioneers whose patient experiments coaxed the first crude automobiles into reluctant life had no idea of the revolution they were unleashing. They were just trying to provide a better alternative to the horse.

Experiments soon gave way to entrepreneurs as the potential of this new means of locomotion was

1992 Nazca C2, potential Italian design for the future.

realised. Legislators, on the other hand, took an early dislike to motor vehicles, which gave the individual citizen unprecedented freedom to travel, and hedged its use round with new restrictions and taxes.

But the tide was unstoppable and a new industry was born. Since the first sale of a car to a customer at the end of the 1880s, some 5000 car manufacturing companies have gone into — and mostly out of — production, yet despite this high rate of attrition, several of the world's leading car producers have been in business since the very dawn of motoring.

Successes and failures, all have interesting (and sometimes incredible) histories: cars have been built by hatters, pork-butchers, mouth-organ salesman and makers of voting machines; one of the world's larger makers began as a manufacturer of cork products!

Throughout those hundred motoring years, failure has played a necessary counterpoint to success; for every Henry Ford who has built cars by the million there have been hundreds of bold venturers who have enjoyed a brief moment of glory and then vanished from the scene forever, leaving a few orphan vehicles to mark their passing.

But such is the magic of the motorcar that even such waifs have found their partisans: collecting antique motorcars has been a hobby (and for some a passion) for more than 60 years, and a typical rally of veteran, vintage or classic cars will have its fair sprinkling of lost causes. Watch the annual London to Brighton Veteran Car Run, the world's most popular motoring event, and you will see survivors of dozens of long-dead marques.

Their longevity proves that it's not always the bad cars that fail; in the motor industry the difference between success and failure has often been razor-thin and the fate of a company has sometimes hung on as fine a margin as the arrival of a modest cheque in the post — that was certainly the factor which ensured the survival of the infant Ford Motor Company back in the summer of 1903...

Aided by a select team of international specialists, I wrote the first edition of this encyclopedia back in the late 1970s when the world was recovering from the first great oil shock. In the intervening years, the car industry has changed dramatically, though it's too soon to say whether for better or worse. All that is certain is that the next hundred years will be just as full of change and surprises as the first century of motoring has been!

David Burgess Wise 1992

Prehistory ¹

MAN'S SEARCH FOR some form of motive power to replace the horse goes back over 300 years; clockwork, wind power and elaborate clockwork gearing were all tried before the power of steam became tractable enough to be used to drive a vehicle. Not that it was initially too successful: the oldest surviving self-propelled vehicle, Cugnot's 1770 *fardier*, owes its preservation to the fact that on its trial runs it ran amok and knocked down a wall! Put into store, it survived the French Revolution, was acquired by the Conservatoire des Arts et Métiers in Paris in 1799, and has been a major exhibit there ever since.

It was followed by a number of even less practical designs from optimistic French, English and American engineers, and it was not until 1801 that the first successful road carriage appeared. This was the work of the Cornish mining engineer Richard Trevithick and led to his London Carriage of 1803, which made a number of successful runs in the capital before it was dismantled to power a hoop rolling mill. Trevithick lacked the staying power to perfect either this or his other great invention, the railway carriage. He was succeeded by a lunatic gaggle of inventors who proposed machines driven by articulated legs, tiny railway engines running inside a drum like squirrels, compressed air, gunpowder and 'vanes, or fliers, like the sails of a windmill'.

Then, between 1820 and 1840, came a golden age of steam, with skilled engineers devising and operating steam carriages of advanced and ingenious design; men like Gurney, Hancock and Macerone all produced designs which were practicable, capable of achieving quite lengthy journeys and operating with a relatively high degree of reliability. Walter Hancock, a better mechanic than businessman, operated his steam coaches on regular scheduled services in London in the 1830s, but was rooked by his associates, and eventually called it a day after 12 years of experiment had brought him little more than unpaid debts and the hostility of those with vested interests, who, fearing that the steam carriage would prove a threat to the thousands whose livelihood depended on the horse, promoted swingeing tolls on the turnpike roads; an 1831 Parliamentary Commission, though largely favourable to the steam carriage, failed to prevent such injustices, and the final blow to the builders of steam carriages came with the advent of the railway age. Railway engines, running on smooth, level rails, had none of the problems experienced by steam carriages running on uneven, badly maintained roads, and this newer form of locomotion soon eclipsed the steam carriage, even though legislation restricting the speed and operation of steam carriages was not enacted until 1863, when it was decreed that all 'road locomotives' should have a man with a red flag walking ahead.

It was the advent of the bicycle in the 1860s which revived touring by road.

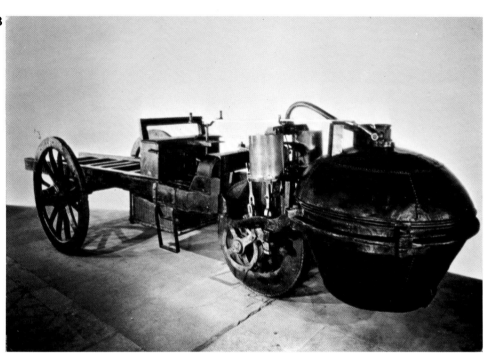

Some of the successes and failures of the prehistory of motoring: James's steam carriage (**1**) was one of the better road carriages of the early 1830s, while Dr Church's Birmingham Road Carriage (**2**) was never completed in this baroque style. The 1770 Cugnot (**3**) is the world's oldest self-propelled vehicle to survive, though it is possible that it never ran. Johann Hautsch of Nürnberg devised this curious clockwork carriage (**4**) in the seventeenth century, while the Hancock steam drag of *c*.1830 (**5**) represents the high point of early British steam carriages.

Radiators

The earliest cars, which, if they even had radiators to cool their engines, had them slung at the rear of the chassis or some other anatomically improbable position, lacked a certain amount of character. When, however, Mercedes developed the honeycomb radiator into a recognizable marque symbol, cars began to acquire personality. And, despite the hiding of the radiator behind a grille, it is still front end treatment that gives a car its character.

When Ettore Bugatti originally adopted a shape for the radiators of his cars (1), he apparently followed the outline of a chairback designed by his furniture-designer father, Carlo. The 1949 Bristol 400 (2) took its functional radiator openings from the BMW with which it was closely connected. Typical of its era, the 1913 Unic radiator (3) reflects honest craftsmanship, while the flamboyant frontal treatment of the 1959 Ford Fairlane Skyliner (4) is a product of a time when the stylist was king. On the other hand, the 1936 Railton (5) cloaked its American origins behind a very English radiator.

6

7

NH 3610

8

JTR 867

10

Like an Art Deco fencer's mask, the radiator grill of the 1936 Triumph Dolomite (**6**) is one of the more extreme designs of a decade when styling began to influence sales. But the crude front end of the 1921 Carden cyclecar (**7**) is purely a dummy, aping larger cars. The 'dollar grin' of the 1947 Buick Eight (**8**) celebrates an age of promise (of increased sales!) after World War Two; over 20 years on, a new era of restraint is marked by the bland front end of the 1970 Monteverdi 375L (**9**). The Rolls-Royce radiator (**10**) has remained true to its original design concept for over 75 years.

1880 to 1900

THE INTERNAL COMBUSTION engine appeared early in the history of the motor vehicle, but took over three-quarters of a century to be perfected to the level where it could be used in a vehicle capable of running on the roads—the 1805 powered cart of the Swiss Isaac de Rivaz was no more than an elaborate toy, only capable of crawling from one side of a room to another, and the 1863 car built in Paris by J-J. Etienne Lenoir took three hours to cover six miles. It was not until the mid-1880s that the first successful petrol cars appeared, developed independently by two German engineers, Gottlieb Daimler and Karl Benz.

Of the two vehicles, that of Benz was incontestably superior, for it was designed as an entity, using the new technology of the cycle industry, while Daimler's carriage was no more than an adapted horse vehicle. Benz went into limited production of his three-wheeled carriages (described in his catalogue as 'an agreeable vehicle, as well as a mountain-climbing apparatus') in 1888; Daimler was more interested in selling his engines as a universal power source.

Neither man found immediate success, but neither had the great geniuses of the steam vehicle who were their contemporaries. The Bollée family of Le Mans built some truly advanced steam carriages between 1873 and the mid-1880s, vehicles which pioneered independent front suspension, while blacksmith's son Léon Serpollet conceived the 'flash boiler' for instantaneous generation of steam and held the first driving licence issued in Paris. And while the Comte De Dion and his engineers Bouton and Trépardoux built some excellent steam vehicles during the 1880s and early 1890s, they were to achieve their greatest fame as manufacturers of light petrol vehicles, from 1895 on.

The crucial event in the story of the motor car was the 1889 Paris World Exhibition, for it was there that the French engineers Panhard and Levassor saw the Daimler 'Steelwheeler' car powered by the Daimler vee-twin engine. Levassor's lady friend, an astute widow named Louise Sarazin, held the French rights to the Daimler engine in succession to her late husband, and Panhard and Levassor began manufacturing these power units in 1890. They could, however, see no future for the motor car, and so granted the right to use Daimler engines in self-propelled vehicles to the ironmongery and cycle firm of Peugeot (who had just decided not to go ahead with the planned production of Serpollet steamers).

It was in France, too, that Benz enjoyed his first limited success, for his Paris agent, Emile Roger, managed to sell one or two Benz cars in Paris (and, coincidentally, garaged his first Benz in Panhard and Levassor's workshop). But it was not until his first four-wheeler, the 1893 Viktoria, that Benz began series production.

Peugeot were already established as motor manufacturers by that date, for in 1891 they had

De Dion, Bouton and Trépardoux built this neat little steam car in 1885 (**1**); the lordly Bollée *Mancelle* steam carriage of 1873 (**2**) was a precursor of petrol car design, with the engine under a frontal bonnet driving the rear wheels, and independent front suspension. Indeed, the 1899 Fiat 3½hp (**3**) and its contemporaries were far more primitive in concept. The first petrol car conceived as an entity was the 1885–86 Benz three-wheeler (**4**). Serpollet's 1888 three-wheeler (**5**) used his high-speed flash boiler. The 1895 tricar (**6**) utilized the power unit from a Leyland steam lawnmower.

Couched in glowing Victorian prose, this advertisement (**left**) is, in fact, a pastiche conceived for Daimler's 40th anniversary in 1936! Built by a firm once famed for sewing machines and cycles, the 1898 Hurtu (**below**) (whose name did nothing to recommend the marque to timorous English motorists!) is a typical horseless carriage.

actually sold 5 cars, boosting production to a dizzy 29 the following year.

The success of the Peugeot cars inspired Panhard and Levassor to reconsider their early opinion of the horseless carriage, and, after building a couple of crude dogcarts with the engine at the rear, Levassor devised the famous *Système Panhard*, with the engine at the front driving the rear wheels via a sliding pinion gearbox inspired by the mechanism of a lathe, a layout which, however '*brusque et brutale*' its inventor thought it, has been used on the majority of motor cars built since.

In America, the motor car was evolving along different lines from Europe and, in January-February 1891, the New World's first petrol vehicle, a friction-driven three-wheeler built by John W. Lambert of Ohio City, made its first tentative runs. In 1895, America's first motor manufacturing company was founded by the Duryea brothers, Charles and Frank (whose prototype dated from 1893); the following year they exported a couple of vehicles to Britain. However, anti-motoring prejudice in that country was running high, and there was little encouragement for motor vehicles, either home-grown or imported (though the company promotions of the so-called 'father of the British motor industry', H. J. Lawson, succeeded in parting a good many credulous investors from a large amount of cash).

Lawson had influential friends and in 1896 succeeded in getting the ridiculous requirement for motor cars to be preceded by a man on foot (a legacy of the old Locomotives on Highways Acts of 1865 and 1878) to be repealed, and held a commemorative run to Brighton on November 14, 1896 to celebrate the raising of the speed limit to 12 mph. Some of the participating machines, though, covered the distance by train and were cosmetically muddied after they had been unloaded, and the first machine home, a Duryea, was not one of the marques under Lawson's aegis (he had expensively purchased a great number of motor car patents in a forlorn effort to monopolize the nascent British car industry).

Demand for motor cars was growing steadily during the latter part of the 1890s, and by now the Benz had become the world's most popular car, with the 2000th production vehicle being delivered in 1899. Motoring was still the sport of a few rich eccentrics, however, and many people had never seen a car.

It was to remedy this defect that, in 1900, the Automobile Club of Great Britain and Ireland held its famous 1000 Miles Trial, which took in most of the major cities of England and Scotland. A total of 65 cars, many English Daimler and MMC models built by Lawson's empire, set out from Hyde Park Corner, London, in April; the major part of this entry finished the run without major mishap, proving that the motor car had at last become a reliable—or relatively so—touring vehicle after a century's gestation.

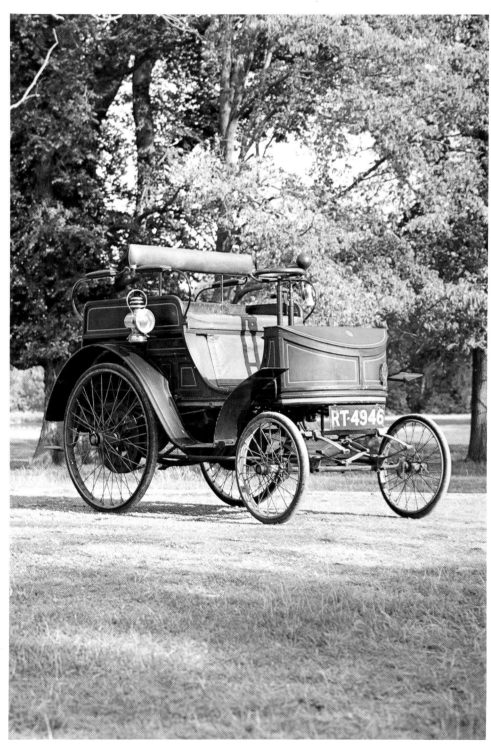

Badges and mascots

Radiator badges were the heraldry of the early motor car. Starting as simply makers' plates fixed to the radiator, badges quickly developed into a minor art form. Some badges, indeed, were masterpieces of the enameller's craft; the Invicta was endowed with a polychromatic butterfly badge delicate enough for jewellery. As for mascots, they began as good luck charms like teddy bears tied to the radiator, but soon the techniques of statuary were being employed to produce mascots of real beauty. The Hispano stork and the Rolls-Royce 'Spirit of Ecstasy' became marque symbols, though owners also commissioned individual mascots, like the Wagnerian soprano whose Métallurgique was endowed with a sterling silver Seigfried clad in chain mail.

(1) The Calometer temperature gauge, a popular 1920s accessory, on a 1927 Morris-Cowley. (2) Packard's emblem – 'a pelican in her piety'. (3) A one-off mascot on a Cadillac V-8. (4) The Hotchkiss badge recalls the firm's origin. (5) A 1914 Star 15.9hp. (6) Jaguar's mascot, derived from a sculpture by motoring artist Gordon Crosby. (7) The Armstrong Siddeley sphinx.

1901 to 1914

THE NEW CENTURY was spectacularly ushered in by 'the car of the day after tomorrow', the Mercedes, designed by Daimler's engineer, Wilhelm Maybach. The contract to produce the first batch of 30 cars had been signed within a month of Gottlieb Daimler's death in March 1900. They had been ordered by the wealthy Austro-Hungarian Consul at Nice, Emil Jellinek, who insisted that they be christened after his daughter Mercédès, a name which found such favour with the wealthy car-buying public that all German Daimler cars were soon known as 'Mercedes', too.

The advanced design of the Mercedes, which combined in one harmonious whole elements such as the honeycomb radiator, pressed steel chassis and gear-lever moving in a gate rather than a quadrant, 'set the fashion to the world' and soon many high-priced cars were copying its layout; even comparatively small cars like the Peugeot were built on Mercedes lines.

These cars did not, however, represent the 'popular motoring' of the early 1900s; this was the province of single-cylinder runabouts like the De Dion and the Renault—again, these well-built cars were widely imitated—and, in America, first by light and temperamental steam cars like the Locomobile and then by gas buggies, of which the most famous was the Curved-Dash Oldsmobile.

But the development of the motor industry in America was being hampered—as it had in Britain a few years earlier—by the shadow of monopoly. A patent lawyer named George Baldwin Selden had drawn up a 'master patent' for the motor vehicle in 1879, published it in 1895 and claimed that all gasoline-driven vehicles were infringements of that patent. His claims were eventually given commercial teeth by the Association of Licenced Automobile Manufacturers, established to administer the Selden Patent in 1902, to which most major American car firms were persuaded to belong.

However, Henry Ford, who founded his Ford Motor Company in June 1903, decided to stand against the ALAM, who began proceedings against him in 1904. After lengthy litigation, which resulted in the ALAM building a car to Selden's 1879 design and Ford building a car with an engine based on that of the 1863 Lenoir, Ford won the day in 1911—not long before the Selden Patent would have expired anyway—but the victory established him as a folk hero.

Ford's great achievement, after five years' work, was to introduce in October 1908 the immortal Model T, which became so popular that he was forced to introduce the car industry's first moving production line in order to build enough cars to satisfy demand. His 'Universal Car' changed the face of motoring; over 16·5 million were built before production ended in 1927, truly 'putting the world on wheels' and transforming the face of society.

A 1901 Curved-Dash Oldsmobile

Though the Edwardian era saw motoring become more popular, on the other hand it also saw the finest and most elegant cars of all time, built to a standard of craftsmanship which could never be repeated. After World War One, many of the great marques faded away in a genteel decline: Delaunay-Belleville, 'the Car Magnificent', the favourite marque of the Tsar of Russia and one of the very best of the French cars of the pre-1914 era, became just a *petit bourgeois* in the 1920s.

Napier, the British company which popularized the six-cylinder engine, enjoyed perhaps even greater acclaim than its rival, Rolls-Royce, while its sales were controlled by that bombastic character Selwyn Francis Edge; when Napier gave him a £160,000 'golden handshake' after a dispute over policy in 1912, however, the company's fortunes seemed to leave with him. Edge, having agreed to leave the motor industry for seven years, became a successful Sussex pig-farmer; Napier built very few cars after the war, concentrating instead on its aero engines.

Such ostentatious machinery relied for its existence on a pool of highly skilled, lowly paid craftsmen with a surpassing pride in their work; against the onslaught of cheap machines produced in America by unskilled labour using production techniques which eliminated most of the human factor, the big luxury cars stood little chance. They represented only a tiny fraction of the potential market for the motor vehicle and, even if their production had not been decimated by the drying up of the car market as a result of the war, they would inevitably have died out as a result of the social changes in the post-war world.

Europe, indeed, experienced an outburst of popular motoring in the 1910–14 period which owed nothing to American concepts of mass production; instead, it grew out of the motorcycle industry, whose engines, single-cylinder or vee-twin, offered lightness and power. Optimistic enthusiasts installed these engines in chassis of often suicidal crudeness, with cart-type centre-pivot steering in many cases, as well as other unmechanical devices such as wire cables coiled round the steering column instead of a conventional steering box and drag link, belt and pulley transmission and tandem-seat layouts with the driver in the second row of the stalls. These crude devices, known as cyclecars, flourished especially in England and France; attempts to transplant them to America failed because they were simply unsuited to the very different motoring environment there.

The worst of the cyclecars were short-lived, however; the designs of the late Edwardian period which promised perhaps the most for the future were the new light cars like the Morris-Oxford, the Standard and the Hillman, all 'big cars in miniature' of around 1100cc, with four cylinders and built on proper engineering lines. These admirable machines were to be the pattern for the popular family cars of the 1920s.

One of the great names of motoring in the Edwardian era was Napier: this 1907 60hp six-cylinder (1) has been constructed as a replica of the car on which S. F. Edge averaged over 60mph for 24 hours to inaugurate the Brooklands race track. This 1903 Fiat 16/20hp (2) was shown at the Agricultural Hall Exhibition in London: its Grosvenor tonneau body is English-built. The popular impression that motor cars were 'engines of death' is illustrated by this 1904 cartoon (3); a more idealized concept of motoring is shown in the 1908 Argyll advertisement (4).

Another, if humbler, 'immortal' of the period was the twin-cylinder Renault AX (**5**), for this chassis was used on the taxis which ferried troops to the Battle of the Marne and saved Paris in 1914. Some of the ignorant fear of motoring may have been caused by the strange garb affected by early motorists, like these sinister anti-dust masks (**6**), from 1907.

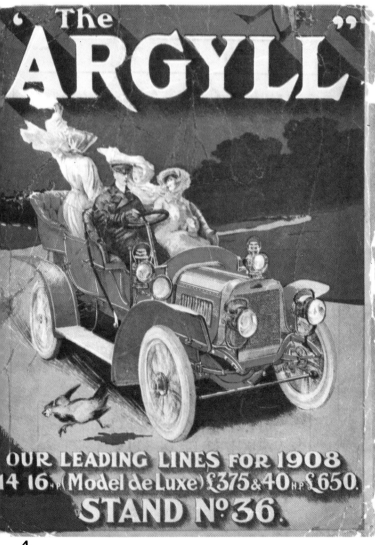

The "ARGYLL"

OUR LEADING LINES FOR 1908
14·16·H.P. (Model de Luxe) £375 & 40 H.P. £650.
STAND N° 36.

4

6

Wheels

1

The wheel is one of man's most fundamental inventions, as it has no parallel in nature. The earliest cars rolled into the world on wire wheels derived from cycle practice, or on wooden wheels developed from those used on carriages. These basic types have been followed by many different patterns of wheel: only the roundness has remained constant.

The wire wheels of the 1898 Hurtu (1) are typical of those used on many early light cars. Their spindly construction makes them unsuitable for high speed. One of the odder inventions of Edwardian times was this hub-mounted tyre pump (2), here fitted to a wooden-wheeled Gladiator. Wooden artillery wheels (3) were common on most pre-World War One European cars, and were still being used in America throughout the 1920s. Bugatti's famous spoked aluminium wheels (4) were developed for racing use. Cheap to make and light in weight, they could be changed complete with brake drum.

The spokes on the wheels of this Model A Ford (**5**) are electrically welded to the rim, not located by adjustable nipples as on conventional wire wheels. The wheels on this 1923 Calcott (**6**) are pressed steel simulating wooden artillery wheels, a popular fashion on British light cars of the 1920s. Wheeltrims have ranged from vulgar (**7**) to the elegantly practical (**8**), the latter being used to protect a wire-spoked wheel and make it easier to clean. Styling of wheels is nothing new —compare the Bugatti of the 1930s (**9**) with the Toyota (**10**).

1915 to 1930

THE TECHNOLOGY of the motor age revolutionized the way that World War One was fought. The internal combustion engine gave new mobility to the infantry who, before hostilities in Europe came to a standstill in the trenches, could be rushed to reinforce weak points in the front line (most notably when the French General Gallieni sent 6000 reinforcements to repel Von Kluck's attack on Paris in 1914); it also provided motorcycles for despatch riders, permitted H. G. Wells's forecast of 'land ironclads' to be fulfilled in the angular shapes of the first armoured cars and tanks and, perhaps most significantly, gave warfare a new dimension by taking it into the air.

One way and another, most of those who fought in the war were given an insight into the utility of the motor vehicle, and when peace came many returning soldiers were only too anxious to spend their demobilization pay on a car of their own. The result was a boom such as the motor industry had never known. Especially in Britain and France, the established manufacturers found themselves contending for the favours of the car-buying public with a whole new sub-industry of optimists who, working from inadequate back-street premises, assembled light cars and cyclecars from proprietary components in the hope that they might make their fortunes. Most found only commercial failure, like the British firm who, with the bailiffs mounting a 24-hour watch outside the doors of their London factory, broke an exit through the unguarded rear wall, loaded as much of their machinery as possible on to the finished chassis and drove off to seek new (but unforthcoming) fortune in the Midlands.

If the American industry had already developed to the extent where success in popular car sales would inevitably go to the established big battalions (even Chrysler, founded in 1924, sprang from the established Maxwell-Briscoe grouping), there was still room in Europe for new mass-producers. Most spectacular of these was André Citroën, a former gear manufacturer, who, with the aim of bringing Ford-style mass-production to France, enjoyed an immediate success with his 10 hp launched in 1919. However, the rise of Citroën spelt doom for the dozens of optimistic assemblers who clustered most thickly in the north-western suburbs of Paris.

The boom collapsed in 1920–21, speeded on its way by strikes, hold-ups, shortages, loss of stock market confidence in the car industry, restrictions on hire-purchase sales, costlier raw materials, and the introduction of a swingeing horsepower tax in Britain.

Only the fittest survived: Ford, whose example was followed by a number of American and European makers, cut prices in order to boost falling sales (though he compensated for

The Blackhawk of 1929 was a short-lived attempt by Stutz to build a lower-priced car.

the loss on the cars by compelling the dealers to take $40-worth of spare parts on which there had been no reduction) and gained a brief respite, though even he had to close down for some months to clear unsold stocks. It was not until 1922 that the motor industry was back on course and a second generation of post-war popular cars began to emerge, most notably the Austin Seven.

Many of the cars of the 1920s profited from the technology of the aero engines developed during the war, most notably the overhead camshaft Hispano-Suiza V-8. Wolseley built this engine under licence and used an overhead camshaft on their post-war cars, but it was not until after the 1927 takeover by Morris that this Wolseley design realized its full potential, especially in MG sports cars.

Hispano-Suiza put their aero engine expertise to full account in the 1919 32cv of 6·6 litres, a splendid machine with servo-assisted four-wheel brakes and delightful handling characteristics, whose overall conception was several years ahead of any of its rivals.

Bentley, who had built rotary aero engines during the war, brought out an in-line four with an overhead camshaft in 1919 (though it was not put into production until 1921); this 3-litre was to become one of the immortal sporting cars.

Many leading manufacturers adopted the overhead camshaft layout during this period, but Rolls-Royce, whose aero engines had used this layout, stuck resolutely to side valves on their cars until the advent of the 20 in 1922; this had pushrod ohv, a configuration followed on the 1925 Phantom which was to supplant the Silver Ghost, which had side valves till the end.

Oddly enough, apart from honourable exceptions like the Hispano, it was the cheaper cars which pioneered the use of brakes on all four wheels, one of the most positive advances in car equipment in the early 1920s. Possibly it was felt that luxury cars would be handled by professional drivers, who would be less likely to indulge in the kind of reckless driving that would require powerful brakes! Moreover, some American popular car makers, appalled at the cost of retooling their cars to accept brakes on the front wheels, actually campaigned against their introduction on the grounds that they were dangerous.

As the decade wore on, more features designed to make motoring more comfortable and safer became commonplace—windscreen wipers, electric starters, safety glass (first standardized on the 1928 Model A Ford), all-steel coachwork, saloon bodies, low-pressure tyres, cellulose paint and chromium plating all became available on popular cars. Styling and the annual model change became an accepted part of the selling of motor cars, bringing with them huge tooling costs which could only be borne by the biggest companies. Many old-established firms just could not keep up and were swept away by the onslaught of the depression in 1929.

Typical of American quality car design in the late 1920s is this 1929 Packard 640 six-cylinder phaeton (**1**). The Hispano H6B (**2**) was one of the great designs of the 1920s. A 1925 aluminium-bodied sports version of the 10.8hp Riley (**3**), normally known as the 'Redwinger'. Two of the most famous popular cars of the era were the Morris-Cowley 'Bullnose' (**4**) and the Model T Ford (**5**). Their very different designs reflect popular taste in Britain and America.

Body styles

Since the dawn of motoring, a bewildering lexicon of words has been used to describe automobile bodywork, many descending from horse-carriage practice, others coined by car manufacturers. Some became standard practice, like the use of the word 'torpedo' to describe an open four-seater touring car; others, like the similar 'gunboat roadster', vanished into limbo. Fashion, too, has played its part in determining names: in America, 'touring' was superseded by 'phaeton' in an attempt to standardize coachwork nomenclature. And, of course, there are the national differences in usage – a 'saloon' is a closed car in England, a public bar in America, where the car becomes a 'sedan'. Henry Ford devised the names 'Tudor' (two-door) and 'Fordor' (four-door) to describe the Model T sedan; after more than 50 years these names are still in use internally in the Ford Motor Company. Today, there is little variation in body styles – most cars are saloons, though 'hatchback' and 'notchback' are specialized subdivisions of the type. Legislation has all but killed off the convertible, save for specialist sports cars, and the word coupé – once used for two-seaters with a folding hood that was normally kept erected – now means any sporting saloon that is lower than average!

The pane of glass ahead of the folding rear roof section of this Fiat Tipo 4 (1) of c.1914 vintage identifies it as a three-quarter landaulette; a landaulette has the rear roof folding from immediately behind the door pillar. A sedan (2) of the traditional pattern is mounted on this 1931 Chevrolet. Chrysler, however, created a new name when they applied wood to the metal panelling of their Town and Country range: this 1949 two-seater (3) emphasizes the 'sporty-formal' ethos of that model. Designed to eliminate body rattles, the Weymann saloon (4), here mounted on a Peugeot, had lightweight wood framing with a leathercloth covering.

Two-seaters of a semi-sporting nature,
like this 1938 Citroën 7cv (**5**), are often known as
roadsters. The 1975 Lotus Elite (**6**) and the wicker-
bodied Bugatti (**7**) show how specialist
manufacturers are free of the styling constraints
imposed on mass-producers. John Tjaarda styled
the 1937 Lincoln-Zephyr V12 (**8**), one of the
pioneering aerodynamic cars.

1931 to 1945

PERPAPS THE MOST significant pointer to the changing status of the motor car can be gauged from the fact that, at the beginning of the 1920s, the majority of cars were open tourers; by 1931, saloon bodies were fitted to 90 per cent of the cars produced. A contemporary editorial sums up the more functional, utilitarian role of the typical 1930s motor car: 'Today there is no room for the cheap and shoddy, or for immature design. The day has passed when unmechanical contraptions can claim the serious attention of the public . . . manufacturers no longer expect the public to carry out the testing of new productions for them'.

However, the public was also calling for smaller engines, more suited to the economic climate of the times. To cope with the weight of saloon bodywork and all the popular accessories, these little engines had to be geared low. Consequently they revved high and hard, and their bores wore alarmingly. The days when durability was a feature taken for granted on all but the shoddiest of cars seemed long past.

The design of cars now began to change radically as well. The demand for more capacious bodywork on small chassis led to the engine being pushed forward over the front axle. The radiator became a functional unit concealed behind a decorative grille which became more elaborate and exaggerated as the decade wore on until on some cars it resembled a chromium-plated waterfall or fencer's mask.

During the 1930–35 period, there was a vogue for streamlining which found its full flower in devices like the Chrysler Airflow, the Singer Airstream and the Fitzmaurice-bodied Ford V-8. Even on more staid cars, the angularity of line that had characterized the models of the late 1920s gave way to more flowing contours. Though most cars still retained running boards, the separate side valances were eliminated by bringing the lower door edges down to give a lower, more bulbous look, accentuated by the adoption of wings with side panels, often blended into the radiator and bonnet.

The swept tails of the new-style coachwork now usually concealed some kind of luggage accommodation as well, a feature sadly lacking on most 1920s models, which usually boasted a luggage grid and nothing more.

'Well-rounded and commodious', the cars of the 1930s offered greater comfort and convenience than their forebears. The stylist, however, had taken over from the engineer and the craftsman bodybuilder and, as a result, the new cars were often deficient in handling as the main masses were now concentrated at either end, like a dumb-bell. New suspension systems— especially independent front springing—also brought their handling problems, and some cars had to be fitted with bumpers incorporating a harmonic damping device to prevent them from

Henry Ford's 'last mechanical triumph' was his 1932 V8, seen here with phaeton bodywork.

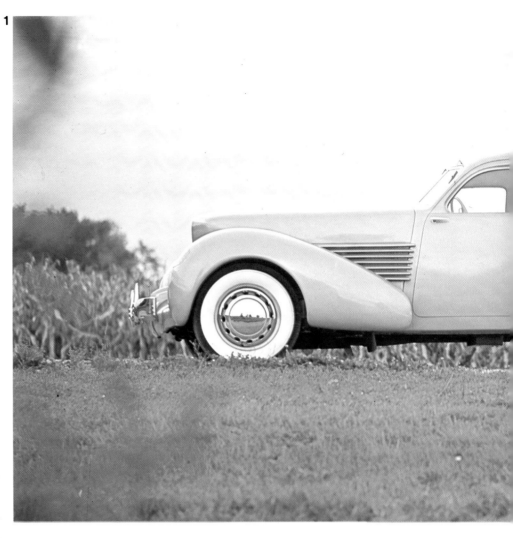

shimmying right off the road on their supersoft springing.

Not that all was gloom and despondency in the 1930s: some manufacturers produced excellent cars during the decade. Morris and Austin continued to build soundly engineered small cars (though Herbert Austin was distinctly upset when his designers insisted on moving the radiator behind a dummy grille, as he felt that it was a kind of heresy), while the last two new models in which Henry Ford was personally involved, the 8hp Model 19Y and the V-8 (both appeared in 1932), were instantly and deservedly successful.

And, of course, there was the famous front-wheel-drive Citroën, which made its debut in 1934. Though its development costs had all but bankrupted André Citroën—who was forced to sell out to Michelin—this was one of the truly great cars.

A lesser, though no less significant, happening was the metamorphosis of the SS marque from a merely meretricious styling exercise into a modestly priced, excellently finished, well-equipped saloon—the first Jaguar.

The same year that the SS Jaguar was launched—1936—Dr Porsche built the prototype Volkswagens, the 'Strength through Joy' cars sponsored by the Nazi Party and intended to be sold to the German public at £50–£55 to keep them from buying imported models—the first of over 20 million of this most popular car of all time. Few Volkswagens, however, were built before the war (though the design was readily adapted for military purposes).

In many ways the 1930s were a watershed—they saw the last of the big luxury cars from makers such as Hispano-Suiza, Duesenberg and Minerva, as well as the end of many small, independent manufacturers and coachbuilders (victims of the swing to mass-produced cars with pressed-steel bodies). The motor industry had reached the point where it had become vital to the economic well-being of the major industrialized countries. Now it was to prove just as vital in providing weapons of war.

In Britain, five of the largest motor manufacturers set up 'shadow factories' in the late 1930s which could be used to produce aero engine parts in the event of war—they were to produce many thousands of aero engines and complete aircraft during the hostilities. Ford joined the five soon after the outbreak of war and was soon building Rolls-Royce Merlin engines on a moving production line in Manchester, while in the USA Ford mass-production expertise was given its greatest test in manufacturing Liberator bombers on a gigantic production line at Willow Run, Michigan.

From the ubiquitous Jeep, through staff cars, trucks, tanks and powerboats to the biggest bomber aircraft, the motor industry played a crucial role in World War Two. Re-adapting to peacetime production was, however, to prove almost as big a test of the industry's abilities.

The 1930s saw a rapid evolution in body design, from traditional shapes like the Zagato-bodied 2.3-litre Alfa Romeo (6) – which nevertheless influenced the styling of many lesser breeds of sports car – to the avant-garde Cord (1) designed by Ray Dietrich and deemed worthy to be shown in New York's Museum of Modern Art. The Type 57 Bugatti (2) has saloon coachwork far more restrained than some of Jean Bugatti's creations on this chassis, while patrician marques like Packard (3) and Rolls-Royce (4) made some concessions to fashion while retaining their innate dignity. So, too, at a more humble level, did the Austin Seven (5).

Engines

Sophisticated and powerful though the engine of a modern car may be, nevertheless it operates on principles first successfully applied over a century ago. The first car engines were simple affairs, usually with one or two cylinders, though since the turn of the century multi-cylinder power units have predominated, normally with four, six or eight cylinders, though non-conformist configurations with three, five, twelve or sixteen cylinders have been tried. Rotary engines have also made sporadic appearances, too. But the main changes in the power unit have been technical improvements: the replacement of the atmospherically operated automatic inlet valve by mechanical inlet valves in the early 1900s, the adoption of monobloc cylinder castings instead of cylinders cast singly or in pairs, the general use of detachable cylinder heads, and the change from side to overhead valves. Today, the overhead camshaft, once the premise of high-powered sports and racing cars, is a common feature of family cars, thanks to the invention of the cogged driving belt, which replaces the complex gear trains of earlier designs and is cheap to install and silent in operation.

Engines developed rapidly: compare the 1908 Hutton (**1**) with its electrolytically-deposited copper water-jackets and dual ignition (the twin carburettors are an anachronism) with the primitive 1900 Benz (**2**) which has an exposed, grease-lubricated crankshaft like its 1885 forebear. The Jaguar XK120 engine, with its twin ohc (**3**) was a classic 1940s design capable of great development, while the 1934 Graham straight-eight, with its centrifugal supercharger (**4**), was a more short-lived way of obtaining increased performance.

6

5

7

8

9

A more modestly priced dohc power unit was the Lotus Twin Cam, here seen in a 1971 Lotus Super Seven (**5**), while the Oldsmobile six in this 1936 Railton (**6**) was a simple side-valve unit relying on good power/weight ratio for performance. In more Wagnerian vein is the 1908 Grand Prix Benz unit (**7**), which promised plenty of 'sturm und drang' with pushrod ohv and drainpipe exhaust. Measure it against the tiny sv engine of the 1936 Morris Eight (**8**) and the powerful American Ford V-8 of the 1970 AC Cobra (**9**).

1946 to 1960

Beset by post-war materials shortages and government interference, motor manufacturers nevertheless soon returned to production, inevitably with slightly modernized pre-war models in most cases though some manufacturers did actually manage to produce all-new cars, notably Armstrong-Siddeley in Britain.

Despite shortages of fuel and tyres, there was a vast demand in Britain for cars, but the government forced manufacturers to export half their output, even though these cars had been designed mostly for the very insular requirements of pre-war Britain. To curb the speculators who had been buying new cars and selling them at an inflated profit, purchasers had to sign a 'covenant' guaranteeing that they would not resell for initially one year, later two.

There was much talk of technical developments arising from wartime projects, but devices such as automatic transmission were only generally adopted in America, and reports that hydraulic suspension, or springing by rubber or torsion bars, were about to be adopted on British cars proved to be more than a little premature. Indeed, some makers seemed unready to come to terms with the future, as one report noted: 'Since wind resistance is an important factor in brake performance, streamlining may lead to braking difficulties, as was shown in experiments carried out in France'.

European manufacturers had also the problem of rebuilding war-shattered plant; in France, the industry had lost machine tools, equipment and labour to Germany and suffered much bomb damage. A shortage of sheet steel and tyres also helped to keep production to about a sixth of the 1938 level in 1946–48, though some recovery was apparent by 1949 when the first post-war Salon de l'Automobile was held in Paris and production had risen to about four times the 1938 monthly level.

Other manufacturing countries had similar difficulties, those of Germany being compounded by the division of the country and the replacement of the Reichsmark ($£1 = RM24$) by the Deutschmark ($£1 = DM11.75$), an effective devaluation of around 100 per cent. Nevertheless, the country's most prolific manufacturer, Volkswagen, continued to make progress despite opinions from British experts—and from Henry Ford II—that the VW was too noisy and uncomfortable to be competitive. And though the BMW factory had ended up in the Russian Zone, the first—and only—'war reparation' design to come out of Germany became the BMW-based Bristol 400.

That was only one of the classic sports cars to appear after the war; more famous still was the Jaguar XK 120, with a twin-cam engine reportedly developed during wartime firewatching duty. It made its debut in 1948 along with two, more utilitarian, designs — the Morris Minor and the Citroën 2cv.

A classic post-war sports car, the Jaguar XK 120

Built by the most traditionally minded motor company of all, the Morgan 4/4 (**1**) of the 1950s was little changed in appearance from its ancestor of the mid-1930s. Like all Morgans built since 1910, it had sliding-pillar independent front suspension. The advanced and complex Citroën DS (**2**) supplanted the immortal *traction avant* in 1955. The 1946 Lincoln (**3**) shows how even quality post-war American cars adopted extreme styling for their radiator grilles.

The 1950s saw the motor industry entering a period of traumatic change. Those brave attempts by independent companies like Kaiser and Crosley to carve a foothold in the American market against the corporate giants of the Big Three—Ford, GM and Chrysler—came to nothing, and the most respected of the old-established independents like Packard, Nash and Studebaker were in decline and would soon vanish, either by attrition or by merger. The American car industry had become stereotyped. Its typical product—generally superlatively hideous—had either a six-cylinder engine (often of fairly antique provenance) or a V-8, and boasted excruciatingly named accessories and components like Hi-Fyre or Firedome engines, HydraMatic or UltraMatic transmissions, even FlightSweep styling. This was the era of the exaggerated tailfin and the grinning chrome grille, and the 'performance car' that could only go fast in a straight line. The announcement of small 'compact' cars in 1959 brought, as well as the Ford Falcon and Chrysler Valiant of conventional design, the unorthodox rear-engined Chevrolet Corvair whose unAmerican handling activities ensured that the US industry went straight from nadir to Nader.

There were mergers in Europe, too, like the shotgun wedding between Austin and Morris, a union born out of strife which would lay the seeds of trouble for that British Motor Corporation's ultimate descendant, British Leyland. But, at that time, their products—small family cars—were just what the public wanted. Fuel economy became even more significant after the 1956 Suez War, when petrol was rationed, and the event created a new race of cyclecars, only now they called them 'bubblecars', and many of them came from German firms grounded in the aircraft industry like Heinkel and Messerschmitt.

In the main, these bubblecars were beastly machines whose only merit lay in their economy; their death-knell was tolled by the advent of an epochal design by Alec Issigonis—the 1959 Mini Minor, which gave a new word to the popular vocabulary and heralded a new race of decently engineered small cars with sports car-like handling. Its layout of front-wheel drive and transverse engine was to set the pattern for the coming 20 years and more.

But the 1950s had their glamour cars, too: Britain produced the big Healeys, the Triumph TRs and the first MG to abandon the perpendicular lines of the 1930s, the slippery profiled MGA, even available with a temperamental twin-cam engine; Italy built big, powerful sports cars like the Ferrari America and Super America; France, which had taxed the *grand'routiers* like Delahaye out of existence, introduced the avant-garde Citroën DS; and Germany, once again *persona grata* after its post-war isolation, brought out the unique and distinctive Mercedes 300SL coupé, with its stylish, if not entirely practical, gull-wing doors.

One of the most sought-after sports cars of the 1950s, both then and now, was the 300SL Mercedes (**4**), with its unorthodox gull-wing doors. Cadillac set the fashion for fins in the 1950s: by the 1954 models (**5**) this vulgar trend had reached its peak.

Dashboards

Though the very first cars were devoid of instruments, by 1899 enterprising accessory manufacturers had begun to offer speedometers: 'motor timepieces' soon followed, along with voltmeters, gradient meters, odometers and petrol gauges. The first 'idiot lights' appeared in 1908 in the shape of a patent oil indicating device which glowed white when there was sufficient oil, red when the level was too low. The invention of the dipstick soon rendered this 'Lubrimeter' superfluous. By 1910, there was even an instrument to measure petrol consumption. Some of these ingenious devices, too far ahead of their time to be commercially viable, have been 're-invented' and, in modern form, appear on some of the latest cars.

Compare the traditional approach of the instrument panel on the 1959 R-type Continental Bentley (1) with the modern approach (2) of the 1979 Saab 900 saloon, with padded steering wheel for safety. The 1951 Porsche 356 Speedster's instrument panel (3) reflects the character both of the car and of the era in which it was built.

38

The complex instrumentation of the 1929 Mercedes 38/250 SS (**4**) is appropriate to a high-performance supercharged car, yet its racing ancestor, the 1908 Benz (**5**) has a bare minimum of instruments, most importantly the drip indicator which shows that oil is going to the engine bearings in sufficient quantity. The 1979 Panther J72 (**6**) represents an attempt to blend traditional dash layout with modern safety requirements. In late-1920s American cars, like the 1929 Stutz Blackhawk (**7**), the hand of the stylist appeared to be set against easy interpretation of the instrument readings, a defect shared by the 1959 Chevrolet dash. (**8**) Despite the appearance of digital electronic gauges in the 1980s, classic analogue dials are still favoured, as in the 1992 Bugatti EB 110.

1961 to 1979

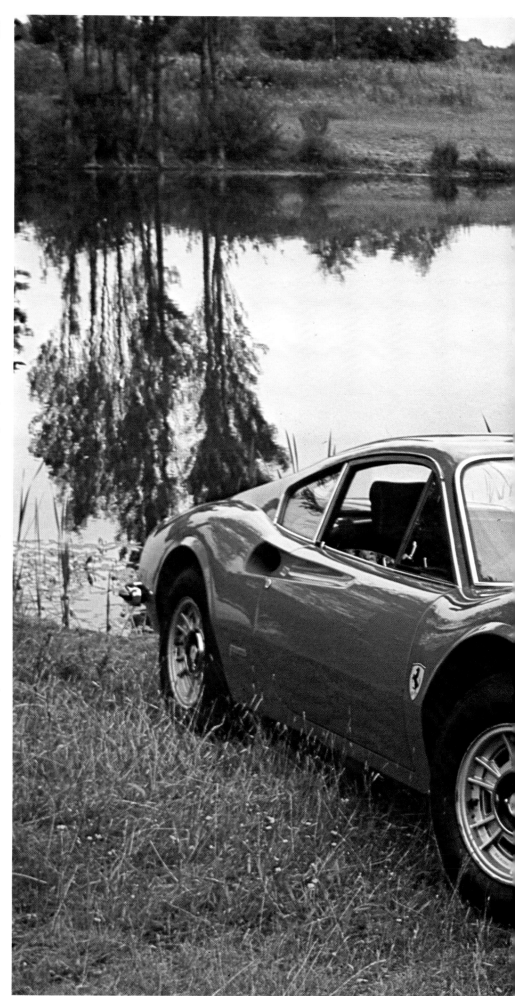

THE VERY SUCCESS of the American compact cars brought new problems to their makers in the early 1960s. For, instead of capturing a whole new market, they encroached into established sales areas, and American dealers began the decade with upwards of a million unsold 'full-size' cars on their hands. Not only that, but the compacts also hit exports of European cars to the USA, and many dealers just stopped selling foreign cars. The only two makes which really managed to hang on to their American sales were Volkswagen and Renault; interestingly enough, in the late 1970s these two firms were to remain most heavily committed to the USA market, VW opening a plant in Pennsylvania in 1978 which gave them third place in sales in a remarkably short space of time, and Renault tying up a sales deal with AMC (which VW had pushed into fourth place).

America was making its presence felt in Europe, too. Ford of America took control of its English affiliate for a record sum of money, and Chrysler began a step-by-step takeover of the Rootes Group with governmental blessing, the task of sorting out the company's financial problems having been judged beyond the powers of mere government officials.

Mergers were the order of the day, for Standard-Triumph joined up with the Leyland Group in 1960, and the same year Jaguar and Daimler combined. Jaguar-Daimler was itself absorbed by the BMC in 1966, while Leyland took over Rover (which had acquired Alvis). Finally, Leyland and the BMC merged early in 1967, after much hard bargaining (though as a prime reason for the merger had been political rather than commercial, the huge and complex group faced extraordinary difficulties right from the start). The result was British Leyland, which later became BL. The problems it in-herited included model lines which competed with one another, thus reducing group efficiency, and the fact that their most outstanding popular model, the Mini, was being produced at a loss—indeed, it was to reach its twentieth birthday before it showed a profit.

German manufacturers were uniting, too: Mercedes had already linked with Auto-Union-DKW, and Volkswagen and NSU also became part of the same grouping during the decade, while the old two-stroke DKW was succeeded by a revived Audi marque. In France, Citroën took over Panhard, one of the industry's oldest marques, in 1965, but ended car production there two years later.

There were many reasons why Europe's manufacturers were joining together—as well as direct mergers, the decade also saw the start of programmes of cooperation jointly to de-velop components such as engines for the benefit of several makers, who perhaps could

Named after Enzo Ferrari's dead son, the Dino brought Ferrari-style motoring to a wider circle. This is a 1972 model.

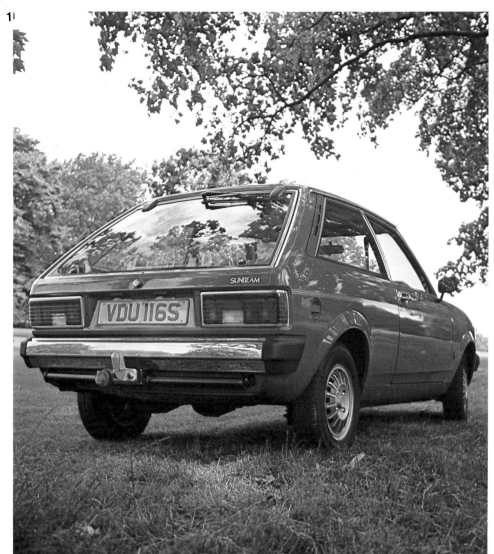

not stand the ever-increasing cost of developing new power plants on their own.

And there was a new source of competition as well, for the Japanese were beginning to send their cars to Europe in small numbers. It was the start of an onslaught which was to become such a torrent that, in little over a decade, manufacturers from some European countries—especially Britain—had to strike a 'gentleman's agreement' with the Japanese manufacturers that the latter would hold down exports to a 'prudent' level, since it was felt that their products were placing too much stress on the indigenous manufacturers. Just how good the Japanese products had become was to be emphasized in 1979, when BL announced that it was to build a Honda model as a stopgap.

A crucial turning point in the history of the automobile came with the Arab embargo on oil exports following the Arab-Israeli War of late 1973. Though supplies were gradually restored to something approaching normality, the system had suffered a shock from which it would perhaps never fully recover, for the era of cheap oil was over.

For America, the experience was particularly traumatic, for the public had become accustomed to unlimited use of big, 'gas-guzzling' cars. Shortages in petrol supply gave Americans a chilling reminder of what life without cars could mean. The eventual result, once panic measures like the virtually overnight switching of production from large models to compacts had subsided, was an almost nationwide blanket speed limit of 55 mph and government insistence on the production of more fuel-efficient cars for the 1980s. There was even, following post-revolutionary cuts in petrol supplies from Iran, the introduction in 1979 of rationing in California, where three-car families were common. This represented a dramatic turnabout in future model policies, and involved vast expenditure. For Ford in 1978, the outlay needed to develop new, more economical cars for the early 1980s fuel consumption limits was greater than the total sum of investment over the company's previous 75 years. For General Motors, it represented an annual bill of $3·2 billion from 1975 on to revise its model range, an increase of 135 per cent on previous years. And for Chrysler, finance had to be found by selling off most of its foreign holdings, notably Chrysler Europe, acquired by Peugeot-Citroën.

Europe had become the focus of the world car industry and by the end of the 1970s was producing some 20 per cent more automobiles than the Americans. But the world industry was poised for an even more dramatic change. The Japanese, having conquered the motorcycle industry with amazing speed, were now poised to take the lead in car manufacturing, too. Motor industry executives began—belatedly—to warn of a 'Trojan Horse' and to attempt to match Japanese productivity levels.

2

3

4

6

A group of cars which epitomizes the face of motoring in the 1970s. The 1978 Chrysler (now Talbot) Sunbeam (**1**) is typical of the modern breed of small hatchback cars. Porsche's 928 (**2**) is one of the ultimate sporting cars, while the Range Rover (**3**), with its go-anywhere four-wheel drive, is a practical workhorse as well as a status symbol leisure vehicle. Oldsmobile's Omega (**4**) is one of their 1980 'X-cars', designed to incorporate more 'European' characteristics than earlier American models. Aston Martin's 1979 V8 (**5**) and the Bertone-styled Fiat X1/9 (**6**) show opposite ends of the sporting scale.

Art and the automobile

Since automobile art first arose in Paris at the turn of the century, mainly taking the form of caricatures and allegorical posters, it has embraced many forms and schools of art, being particularly evident in the contemporary Pop Art and Photo Realism movements in the USA. Popular items for collectors of 'automobiliana' include posters, sculptures, mascots, ornaments, glassware, even 'polychrome sculptural masses' formed from car components fed into a hydraulic press.

An 1898 poster (1) by Belgian racing cyclist Georges Gaudy, this was one of the first posters to advertise a motor race; the car is probably a Benz, and the driver, Old Father Time. More serious artists are painting car subjects today than at any time in the past, and nowhere is this more evident than in the Pop Art and Photo Realism movements; this example of the Photo Realism school is *Wrecking Yard III* (2) by the American Don Eddy. (3) A squared-up drawing and water-colour by Geo Ham (Georges Hamel), a famous French illustrator most active in the 1930s and 1940s.

4

GRAND-PRIX Dieppe
de l'A·C·F·1907

NAZZARO
sur F·I·A·T·

5

6

7

8

The Michelin Tyre Company's building in Fulham Road, London, was the work of architect François Espinasse. Dating from 1910, it is decorated with coloured tiles depicting contemporary racing successes; this scene (4) is of the 1907 French Grand Prix. The Hispano-Suiza catalogue (5) was illustrated by René Vincent, a leading motoring artist from before World War One to the 1930s. (6) Motoring ornaments are widely collected items of 'automobiliana'; this is a porcelain Art Deco example. *Automobilia* (7) is a 1960s Pop Art composition by Peter Philips. (8) A 3.5-litre BMW decorated by American sculptor Alexander Calder, inventor of the 'mobile'.

The evolution of mass production

THE 1980s saw another fundamental shift in the focus of car manufacturing, as the Japanese swept past the American industry in terms of production and made huge inroads into the popular car market on both sides of the Atlantic. Held back in the past by protectionist sales quotas, the Japanese established bridgehead production plants in Europe — particularly Britain — and the United States. By the start of the 1990s, they had fourteen factories in the USA producing one-fifth of all the new cars bought by Americans and were even producing the country's best-selling model. Moreover, they were moving into the luxury car market and challenging the world's best.

In Europe, the opening of new factories was an obvious preparation for the lifting of trade barriers between the member countries of the Common Market at the end of 1992. It will be particularly interesting to see what effect this has on France and Italy, in particular, for in both countries the market has traditionally been dominated by the national producers, who have enjoyed a high level of government protection. Indeed, take away Fiat and its subsidiaries from the Italian market and there is virtually nothing left!

Recently, the car has been under pressure from legislators for its contribution to atmospheric pollution (about 20 per cent in "motorised" countries, 5 per cent worldwide). However, the main sources of harmful emissions — jet aircraft, diesel trains, power stations, factories — have so far largely escaped the expensive solutions imposed on the car makers, who have to spend £10-12 billion

Today, mass-production car factories are making increasing use of computers to control production processes, as in the Fiat works (**below**). However, there has also been a revival in 'traditional' hand production methods for limited-production cars, as in the Panther factory (**bottom and below right**).

annually (half their engineering budgets) on pollution control. In fact, the motor car has been shown to be the most efficient way of moving people, in terms of fuel used, by a significant degree. The exhaust catalysts beloved of legislators notably use more fuel — and actually do not work when the engine is cold this is when 75 per cent of pollutants are produced).

If there was a design theme to the 1980s, it was the growing importance of aerodynamics, which had been around for decades, but suddenly became an important tool in the quest for fuel efficiency. This had become a primary consideration after the dramatic raising of oil prices by OPEC in 1978-79 had coincided with the Iranian revolution in which the pro-Western Shah was toppled by Moslem fundamentalists headed by the Ayatollah Khomeini, effectively cutting off a major source of the West's oil.

On both sides of the Atlantic, Ford — kept afloat only by its successful European operations — gambled with high stakes by switching to an aerodynamic look for its most popular lines. Top management told the designers to create the sort of cars they would like to be seen driving and, though there was initially some reaction from the more conservative customers who dismissed the new cars as "jellymoulds", the new streamlined Fords spearheaded an industry-wide shift to the production of cars that had been formed in the wind tunnel. The results were dramatic. The new streamlined Fords spearheaded a dramatic recovery in the firm's fortunes that led to its profits actually overtaking those of General Motors for the first time in decades.

It was in Europe, however, that Ford made the running in the new global game of takeovers and alliances. In 1984 Ford held discussions with Fiat which, had they come to a successful conclusion,

would have created Europe's biggest automotive grouping; then Ford offered to take over the Austin Rover group, which was all that remained of the former British Motor Corporation, which had undergone a bewildering series of identity changes. As British Leyland in the 1970s, the group had dug itself into deep financial problems through a combination of a ramshackle management structures and a popular car range of perverse ugliness and imperfect reliability. BL had been ill-advisedly bailed out by the government in a vote-catching attempt to preserve jobs in an overmanned group without rectifying the fundamental causes of BL's ills. It remained a steady drain on the national exchequer and an embarrassment to the Conservative government of the 1980s: Ford developed a detailed rationale for the future of Austin Rover, but the plan was scuttled by left-wing sabotage (as was a GM plan to buy Land Rover) and Austin Rover (by now called simply Rover) was taken over by British Aerospace instead.

Ford also attempted to buy the Italian manufacturer Alfa Romeo in 1986: this time it was Fiat which forestalled them, and bought the loss-making Alfa itself.

In the luxury car segment, Ford was more successful, taking over Aston Martin and Jaguar at the end of the decade; denied Jaguar, GM bought Saab on the rebound.

It seemed that such moves only bolstered Fiat head Gianni Agnelli'contention that only four or five independent car manufacturing groups would be left by the turn of the century; and certainly at a lower level, just about every major car maker either owned shares in, or was involved in joint ventures with, companies that were ostensibly its rivals.

As the motor industry approaches the 21st century, it is certain that its future shape will be of even more Byzantine complexity.

Ford led the world in the use of mass production from the first. Here, at Ford's plant in Dagenham (UK), one of the most up-to-date in the global Ford empire, various stages of the process are shown. These include robot studding of the underbody, stages in body assembly, the final highlighting and checking for surface defects and engine timing belt assembly.

How cars are made

THE BUILDING OF A CAR begins with the manufacture of its individual components—up to 15,000 of them. Some of the steel components are forged or cast, but most are made from sheet steel pressed into hundreds of different shapes by huge presses capable of exerting pressures of up to 2000 tons per square inch.

The pressings are carried by fork-lift trucks to the pre-production line workshops, and in separate processes the building of the superstructure and underbody begins. First, small sub-assemblies are put together by spot welding. Then these are fitted into jigs, which hold the pieces in place as they are joined by automatic welders; from these the major superstructure and underbody emerge complete. Modern body

weld units can complete up to 1000 welds simultaneously with absolute accuracy.

Now the doors, plus bonnet and boot lid—all arriving ready-made by overhead monorail conveyor—are fitted. Major panel joints have been gas-welded to give greater strength and flexibility when the car is under stress from cornering or rough roads. Finally the bodywork is prepared for painting; each body shell will be finished in plain or metallic colours to an individual order tapped out by teleprinter.

The car is degreased by high-pressure sprays and phosphated to provide a good anti-corrosion and paint adhesion surface; the body is then stoved. Now the car is totally immersed in an electrocoat primer paint process. This

provides a paint film on all areas of the body, including those box sections which are inaccessible under normal processes. The surplus paint is rinsed off and the body is stoved in a gas-fired oven. All outer joints are sealed before the body passes through electrostatic paint spraying equipment. This automatically applies a grey primer sealing coat, which is then stoved. A protective material is applied to the underbody. Each body is wet sanded, rinsed with de-mineralized water and finally dried. The car is then ready to receive three top coats of enamel paint which is applied manually and stoved in a steam-heated oven.

The cars now move on to the trim shop; each has already acquired an individual identity, and details of its trim specification are transferred from a teleprinter to a card on the bonnet. The build-up starts as components stockpiled beside the production line are fitted—the grille, electrical wiring, lights, head lining, door windows, windscreen.

Then come the under-bonnet parts like horns, battery, brake fluid reservoirs, steering column, radiator and pipes, as well as the instrument panel. Nowadays, much of the complex wiring loom has been eliminated by printed circuits and plug-in modules.

The engine, having been given a 'hot' running test, arrives at the production line complete with carburettors, exhaust manifold, alternator and fan. The clutch/gearbox unit, drive shaft, rear axle, front and rear suspensions—including hubs and brakes—are fitted in a special jig and everything is bolted together. The engine/transmission/suspension assembly moves forward to meet the line from the body shops; the correct body unit is lowered to meet it. The nearly completed car now moves along a raised line. The wipers and interior trim are fitted; the radiator is filled and hydraulic fluid fed into the brake system.

Wheels, made in a separate plant and already fitted with tyres, arrive on a gravity conveyor and are bolted on, and the car rolls forward on its own for the first time. Fuel is added to the tank.

Seats are the last item to be added to the interior. The engine idles as it is checked; then suspension and steering settings are adjusted and checked.

After a final examination of the trim the car undergoes a quality check before it goes on to the roller testing station to test the engine, transmission, steering, brakes and lights. A diagnostic unit checks that the electrical circuit is fully functional. The car is driven on to a conveyorized water test where jets of water at 20 psi are directed on to the cars for four minutes as they pass through the tunnel.

Dried down, it has its final check, then it is parked in the trade compound to await the dealer's delivery conveyor lorries to take it to the showroom.

Developing a new car

THE MANUFACTURE OF A modern popular car is a highly-automated process, making the fullest use of robots and computer technology. In place of the huge stockpiles of components that once dominated car factories, manufacturers now employ a "just-in-time" system, which ensures that parts flow into the factory only as they are needed.

Assembly and testing of power units is increasingly automated: at Ford's engine plant in South Wales, for instance, just 100 production staff can produce 800 engines in every shift. Among the many highly-automated operations is the ingenious use of pneumatic tubes to blow bolts and studs required for engine assembly to automatic assembly tools. While the individual components for the inlet manifold, throttle and fuel injection systems are manually loaded on to platens which supply a special sub-assembly loop, each set of parts is selected according to scheduling instructions issued by the computer which controls the productionlines and assembled by automatic

machines. In all, the Ford engine plant has more than 100 computer-controlled robots and the computer even controls the final test cycle on each complete power unit. The human operator only needs to intervene if there is a problem.

Huge presses stamp out body sides in one piece to ensure maximum precision in manufacture. The outer panels are placed in jigs and tack-welded before robots position and weld the inner panels and wheelarches.

The underbody panels are brought together in multi-welder jigs which give a consistent and extremely accurate performance before robots add the finishing touches to the completed floorpan: the pre-assembled engine compartment is then installed and the complete unit is automatically transferred to a new work station where robots finish the welding and add the studs to which components will be attached.

Computers then select the correct bodystyle for the particular floorplan and robots weld them

together in a "framing buck" before the assembly moves to a second buck for the addition of the roof and scuttle panels: a final welding process completes the body assembly.

For maximum protection against corrosion, vulnerable areas of the bodyshell are now made from zinc-coated steel; the entire shell is then dipped in a bath of protective phosphate paint which is electrolytically deposited into every crevice. Primer and enamel coats are applied by robot spray guns which are informed by the master computer what colour each individual car should be: the days when all the cars on an assembly line had to be painted black so that production was not slowed down are long gone!

After painting, the doors are removed from the car and assembled off-line. Because modern doors contain so many electrical components — motors for the windows, solenoids for the locks, loudspeakers for the in-car entertainment system — this ensures that work can be carried out more accu-

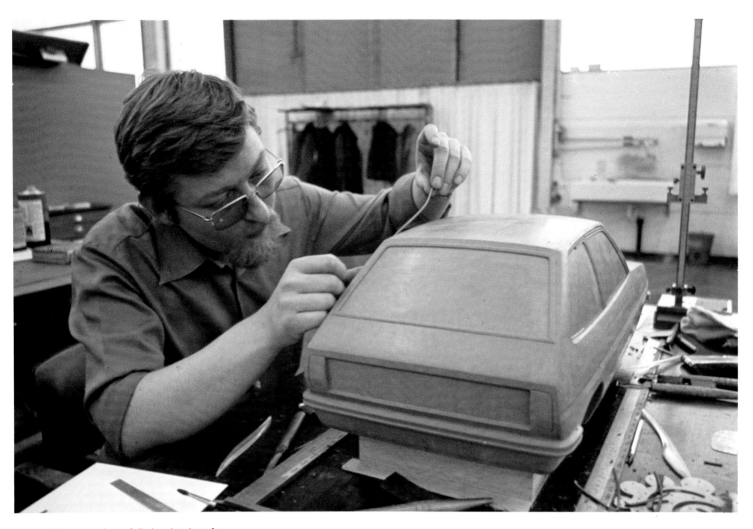

A draughtsman makes a full-size drawing of a
proposed new model so that critical dimensions can
be evaluated (**left**). Because of the cost of building
full-size prototypes, fifth-scale models of a new car
are made so that wind-tunnel tests can be carried
out to 'fine-tune' the aerodynamics before a project
is committed to sheet metal (**above**). Using
modelling clay, highly skilled modellers create not
only full-size mockups of a new design, but also
interior features like the facia panel (**right**).

rately and with less risk of operator fatigue or damge to the paintwork. Then, instead of using manual labour to bolt the door hinges to the body frame, the doors are precisely positioned by sensor-guided robots before automatic welders secure the hinges, eliminating a source of leaks, rattles and wind noise.

Instrument clusters and wiring harnesses, too, are now assembled and tested off-line by robots.

Assembly of the soft trim is becoming increasingly mechanised: headlinings are now preformed pads bonded in place and one manufacturer — Ford — is even moulding seat pads and fabric covering in a single automated sequence that eliminates all stitching, clips and wires.

At the end of the production line, the completed vehicle is given its first shot of fuel, started up and tested using a plug-in diagnostic computer. Hydropulse machines which reproduce the worst road surfaces a vehicle is likely to encounter are used to carry out quality audits and enable possible sources of squeaks and rattles to be identified and eliminated.

It takes around four years to develop the average European-built car. This currently has a production lifespan of some ten years, though, by the early part of the 21st century this could have decreased to four or five. Either way, the car designer has to be able to forecast with some accuracy what will be fashionable and acceptable several years in the future — and make sure that it remains that way for several years more.

A new car generally starts as a designer's concept based on a number of assumptions known collectively as a 'package.' These include the possible power unit, the number of passengers and load-carrying capacity required.

Traditionally, the concept has progressed from sketches to fullsized clay models, but in the past few years computers have completely transformed the design process. Now a designer can create a shape round the package 'hardpoints' on a computer screen with an electronic stylus: once the basic parameters are in place, the computer can develop the design in the round, rotate it for inspection and modification, colour it, make the brightwork sparkle and even show it in animated 'motion' against a simulated background.

The design can be changed, stretched, shortened and revised without anything solid being created; it can even be presented for approval by the company's board, who will be able to see inside and out on the computer screen and view an infinity of alternative concepts. In short, modern computer technology makes it possible to do everything but

Crash behaviour of new models is assessed in controlled tests (**above**), though today much of the information that used to be gained by destroying expensive prototypes can be gained from computer programmes. Unwanted noises can be detected and eliminated by running tests in an anechoic chamber (**left**), a totally soundless environment. Wind-tunnel tests on the completed prototype (**right**) produce much valuable information.

touch and drive the car and progress in virtual reality computer graphics makes that extra step only a short one. It is already possible to crash-test a future car which only exists as a series of electrical pulses in a computer program so accurately that "real-world" testing produces identical results!

Once a concept has been accepted, the computer can control a scanning machine, which can cut a fullsize model of the proposed car from clay or styrofoam, not only for wind tunnel testing but also so that glass fibre moulds can be taken and 'bucks' made for final assessment of interior trim and exterior shape.

Once the design is finalised, the computer can directly transmit its crucial dimensions to the manufacturing area in digitised form, so that machine tools can be programmed and stamping dies cut to form the body panels.

Nowadays design and manufacturing staff work closely together from the earliest stages — a process known as 'simultaneous engineering' — so that a design is not only attractive to look at, but also feasible to manufacture. By cutting down the time spent at the design stage, 'simultaneous engineering' can speed up the introduction of new models and eliminate needless waste.

Computer technology and satellite communication also enables design studios round the world to work simultaneously on the same project. Despite all these advances however, there is one test that cannot be simulated — and that is whether customers will buy the car once it is in the showrooms!

A global industry

THOUGH THE MOTOR industry had its roots in Europe and was subscquently dominatede by the United States, by 1970 Western Europe had once again outstripped the USA. Since then, however, the focus has increasingly shifted to the Pacific Rim countries — most notably Japan, which now boasts the world's biggest manufacturer, Toyota, who overtook General Motors in 1990.

In the 1970s the big European and American manufacturers had moved into new countries and competed with one another for market supremacy: during the 1980s, the tide turned and the Japanese manufacturers began establishing bridgeheads in Europe — where their impact had been previously restricted by import quotas — and in America.

Once they were producing cars by the million, export was essential to the Japanese, for their home market could not absorb all the vehicles they built.

A further new factor was brought into play, by the breakup of the USSR and the collapse of the Communist Party at the beginning of the 1990s, for a potential market of millions, denied cars for decades through enterprise-sapping Socialist dogma and a moribund economy throttled by centralist planning, was opened up virtually overnight. American and European makers were quick to establish a foothold in the former Eastern Bloc countries, for once market forces were unleashed, nobody wanted the crudely made cars that up to then had been all that was available and makes that had been established for decades vanished within weeks.

The World's Leading Car Manufacturers (1990 figures)

▲ AUSTRALIA
▲ BELGIUM
▲ BRAZIL
▲ CZECHOSLOVAKIA
▲ FRANCE
▲ GERMANY
▲ ITALY
▲ SOUTH KOREA
▲ JAPAN
▲ MALAYSIA
▲ MEXICO
   NETHERLANDS
▲ POLAND
▲ RUSSIA
▲ SOUTH AFRICA
▲ SPAIN
▲ SWEDEN
▲ UNITED KINGDOM
▲ USA
▲ YUGOSLAVIA

Rover ▲
397,991
Ford ▲
329,597
Vauxhall ▲
256,293
Ford ▲
336,047
VW ▲
204,300
GM-Opel ▲
389,237
Volvo
121,300
Peugeot ▲
116,548
Nissan ▲
76,190
Jaguar ▲
41,891
Renault ▲
171,936
Volvo ▲
83,122
Trabant
125,000
Porsche ▲
32,162
VW ▲
1,845,780
GM-Opel ▲
937,913
Ford ▲
906,171
BMW ▲
519,660
Mercedes-Benz △
574,395
Audi ▲
421,378
Volvo ▲
254,800
Saab ▲
93,000
VAZ ▲
736,055
IZH ▲
135,000
GAZ ▲
72,000
AZLK ▲
74,000
FSM ▲
210,000
FSO ▲
82,000

Toyota ▲
3,345,885
Nissan ▲
2,020,523
Mitsubishi ▲
833,265
Honda ▲
1,223,389
Mazda ▲
1,118,036
Suzuki △
511,832
Daihatsu ▲
373,110
Subaru ▲
319,585
Isuzu ▲
202,347
Hyundai
225,000
Kia ▲
225,000

Citroen ▲
689,965
Citroen ▲
221,860
Ford ▲
334,418
Autobianchi
144,464 ▲
Fiat ▲
4,368
GM-Chevrolet
8,500 ▲
Ford ▲
10,500
Skoda ▲
187,000
Lancia ▲
168,702
Alfa Romeo
293,643 ▲
Fiat ▲
1,225,410
Proton ▲
85,613

Mitsubishi
45,000 ▲
Toyota ▲
58,378
Nissan ▲
59,764
GM-Holden
110,000 ▲
Ford ▲
137,625

55

Alternative power sources

THOUGH THE FOUR-STROKE internal combustion engine has been around for over a century, it has had remarkably few challengers to its supremacy.

In the early days of motoring, steam and electricity both had their advocates, but their shortcomings led to their general demise. Steam—external combustion—needed a boiler and water tank, and was complex to operate and maintain, while the electric car needed heavy accumulators to give even the most modest of ranges; it enjoyed something of a vogue in America as a town car, however, up to the 1920s.

Once the electric starter was a commonplace item of equipment, the supremacy of the petrol engine was assured, until, that is, fuel shortages inspired manufacturers to search for viable alternatives. During World War One, cars had been run on coal gas carried in bags like embryo Zeppelins, either on the roof or in trailers; during World War Two, private cars were fitted with gas producers generating combustible gas from carbon, usually in the form of charcoal.

Serious development of alternative power sources did not begin, however, until the 1950s. Rover in Britain led the way with production of gas turbine prototypes, and both General Motors and Ford began experiments along these lines. The major American manufacturers also began looking anew at steam and electric vehicles.

Turbines failed to meet the requirements of the car industry, though they had some attraction to truck builders. Their main fault was a 'time-lag' when accelerating; also, their application to mass-produced cars depends on the development of low-cost, high-temperature components designed for satisfactory engine efficiency and performance.

Another candidate which was tried and found wanting was the Stirling 'hot-air' engine, appropriately designed by a preacher in the early 1800s. Powered by a closed-circuit system utilizing heat expansion of an inert gas, the external-combustion Stirling was at one time seriously considered by Ford as a possibility for the production cars of the late 1980s, but the programme got no further than the building of mobile test beds.

Rotary piston engines, long a fruitful field for hopeful inventors, came to the fore with the Wankel trochoidal engine pioneered by NSU in 1963, but failed to stay the course. Though rotaries are more compact than conventional reciprocating engines, they are costlier to produce and maintain, and are not so fuel-efficient.

Even the 'pollution-free' and noiseless electric car has not solved the problems which bedevilled it at the turn of the century. It still relies on heavy storage batteries with limited range, and needs to be recharged at frequent intervals. And, if its batteries are recharged from a conventional oil-fired generating station, the source of the atmospheric pollution is only

Some modern sports cars, like this 1979 Ford Mustang (1), use an exhaust-driven turbocharger for forced induction to obtain greater efficiency from a conventional petrol engine. In the mid-1960s, Ford of Britain developed a small urban electric car prototype, the Comuta (2), but shelved the project in 1967. The most commercially successful 'alternative' engine is the Wankel rotary-piston unit. This is a Citroën-built example (3). The closed-cycle Ford-Philips Stirling 'hot-air' engine (4) was tested in a Pinto car but apparently did not live up to its early promise. The 1990s are seeing many manufacturers experimenting again with electric power. The Blitz Bertone (5) is a 1992 sports car prototype; the Vauxhall Electric Astra (6) is another experiment, here seen being power charged.

transferred from the car to the power station.

One of the more promising alternative power sources is the stratified-charge engine—basically a more efficient variant of the conventional petrol engine. There are two main types, the divided chamber engine and the fuel-injected stratified-charge engine.

The first type is typified by Honda's CVCC engine, which features a dual carburettor and a precombustion chamber, while Ford's PROCO ('programmed combustion') engine represents the second type. This has a special cylinder and piston head design, and uses fuel injectors to deliver a finely atomized spray of fuel directly into the combustion chamber.

But perhaps the most successful 'alternative engine' is also one of the oldest, the diesel, first devised in the 1890s. Long proven in trucks, by the late 1970s diesels were appearing in a small VW family car, the Golf. Able to run on cheaper, less volatile oil fuel than the petrol engine, and of proven longevity, the compression ignition diesel engine only suffered by comparison, as it tended to be harsher-running and less lively. However, it holds great hope for the future.

Cars of the future

Tomorrow, as far as the motor industry is concerned, comes every motor show. But, like good card players, motor manufacturers never reveal every card in their hands when they unveil those glamorous concept cars, designed to reveal the future shape of motoring. Rather, these eye-catching models are pointers to features that might appear on future models, a method of promoting new powerplants or a simple way of testing public reaction to new bodystyles or accessories.

'Dream cars' have been a potent force in guiding and monitoring public taste ever since General Motors' larger-than-life styling chief Harley Earl unveiled his famous Buick Y-Job in 1938 to educate the public to the forthcoming fullwidth body styles.

Today's dream cars look ahead to the next cen-tury, with safety and environmental protection key issues. Good aerodynamics, the big theme of the 1980s, are now taken as normal: the ability to rec-ycle components when the car's useful life is over is becoming increasingly important, particularly as more lightweight materials — particularly plastics — are used to reduce fuel consumption.

As road become increasingly congested, new ways of avoiding accidents are being investigated: among them are a cruise-control incorporating sensors that maintain a safe distance between vehi-cles relative to their speed, a system which warns drivers when their vehicles cross a lane marker without signalling (the idea is to prevent accidents caused by drowsiness or inattention) and a compu-terised guidance system, which controls steering, throttle, brakes and transmission to automatically back the car into its garage.

Satellite navigation systems are increasingly seen on concept cars, and "drive-by-wire" com-puter control of throttle and gearshift uses tech-nology already in service on the most modern jet aircraft.

Over the years, many new power plants — from engines running on hot air to small nuclear reactors — have been proposed on concept cars, but the good old recipocating internal combustion engine remains virtually universal. Ford has been involved in the development of an engine largely made from plastics, which is said to be quieter and have 20 per cent lower emissions than a conventional engine. Another field of experiment involves the 'Orbital' engine, a lightweight valveless three-cylinder two-stroke with low emission levels and improved power and fuel economy: it is expected that the first Orbital-engined cars will be in production by the year 2000.

Only one maker — Mazda — has persisted with rotary-piston engines: electric cars still suffer from restricted range and performance, and, while their engines are fume-free, the power stations which generate the electricity to charge their batteries are usually anything but: it would be rash indeed to predict future developments here.

Hybrid vehicles are one possibility: a small internal combustion engine and alternator can extend the operating range of an electric vehicle to at least 250 miles.

What will tomorrow's car look like? The evidence is that it will have a shorter bonnet, thanks to more compact power units, more glass area, far more space for people and luggage, and less front and rear overhang.

Changing lifestyles — more wealth and leisure, a slowing birthrate, increased life expectancy — are creating new "niche" markets. These could include so-called "multi-purpose" vehicles which combine the space of a minibus or light van with car-type performance, meeting all the needs of a family in a single vehicle and "speciality" cars which offer the style and performance that affluent 'empty nesters' are seeking to recapture after years of prosaic family transportation.

Three of the industry's experimental cars — the Ford Probe (**right**), a prototype from Audi (**below**) with all aluminium body and the GM Ultralite (**left**).

Founders of the motor industry

APPERSON, Edgar *(1870–1959)* **and Elmer** *(1861–1920)*
Collaborated with Elwood Haynes to build one of America's first cars in 1894, later forming Haynes-Apperson. After they broke with Haynes, they founded the Apperson Brothers Motor Car Company.

Herbert Austin

AUSTIN, Herbert *(1866–1941)*
Briton who worked for the Wolseley Sheep Shearing Company in Australia, then returned to England to build the first Wolseley car (1895). Left Wolseley to found Austin (1906), where landmark designs included the Seven and the 12/4. He was knighted in 1917 and became Lord Austin in 1936.

BENTLEY, Walter Owen *(1888–1971)*
Trained as a railway engineer, fitted some of the first aluminium pistons to DFP cars in 1914. After building aeroengines during World War One, he launched the Bentley car in 1919. He later worked for Lagonda.

Karl Benz

BENZ, Karl *(1844–1929)*
Began development of a petrol engine in 1878, founding Benz & Co. in 1883. Built his first motor car in 1885–86, the first petrol car conceived as a unity and owing nothing to horse-drawn carriages.

BIRKIGT, Marc *(1878–1953)*
Swiss engineer who moved to Spain, and became designer of Hispano-Suiza cars and aeroengines.

BOLLÉE, Amédée *père* *(1844–1916)*
French bell-founder and designer of steam carriages which pioneered independent front suspension and other technical features well ahead of their time.

BOLLÉE, Amédée *fils* *(1867–1926)*
Began with steam carriages, but turned to petrol cars in 1896, building a streamlined racer in 1899 with underslung chassis, rear-mounted twin carburettor, and four-cylinder engine with hemispherical combustion chambers.

BOLLÉE, Léon *(1870–1913)*
First achieved fame with the invention of a calculating machine, then, in 1895, devised a sporting tandem-seat voiturette. In contrast, from 1903 he built refined and silent quality cars of advanced design.

BRISCOE, Benjamin *(1869–1945)*
Founded, with Jonathan Maxwell, the Maxwell-Briscoe Motor Company in 1903, and in 1910 organized the United States Motor Company, a combine of some 130 firms, which folded in 1912. In 1913 Briscoe began building cars under his own name. A visit to the 1912 London Motorcycle Show introduced him to cyclecars, which he built in France and America in conjunction with his brother Frank *(1875–1954)*.

BROWN, Sir David *(born 1904)*
Industrialist, who bought Aston Martin and Lagonda in 1947. His backing, which until 1972 ensured the survival of both these famous marques and brought Aston Martin victory at Le Mans.

BUGATTI, Ettore *(1881–1947)*
Born in Milan, he was designing for De Dietrich before he was 21, moved to Mathis, and in 1910 built the first Bugatti car at Molsheim (Alsace). 'Le Patron', rarely seen without his bowler hat, also affected digitated shoes.

BUICK, David Dunbar *(1855–1929)*
Applied the money he made from the invention of the enamelled bathtub to the development of a car engine with ohv. He then, in 1903, organized the Buick Motor Car Company with backing from the Briscoe brothers, but was bought out by Billy Durant late in 1904.

David Buick

CHADWICK, Lee Sherman *(1875–1958)*
Built his first car in 1899, joining Searchmont in 1900. His Chadwick company lasted from 1903 to 1911, and his racing cars pioneered the use of superchargers. His latter years were spent as the head of a stove company.

CHAPIN, Roy *(1880–1936)*
Started with Olds, then, in 1906, helped found Thomas-Detroit (later Chalmers). In 1909 he organized, along with Howard Coffin, the Hudson Motor Car Company. He was an active crusader for better roads for America.

CHAPMAN, Colin *(1928–1982)*
English designer/constructor of Lotus sports and racing cars.

CHARRON, Fernand *(1866–1928)*
French cycle and car racer who collaborated (with Girardot and Voigt) in the CGV car, having made a 'killing' from holding the sole agency for Panhard-Levassor at a time of great demand. Sold his share of Charron Ltd. (as CGV became) to work for his father-in-law, Adolphe Clément, but they split up and Charron eventually built the 'Alda' car. Though he was very bald, the fashionable M. Charron rarely wore a hat, a matter for some comment at the time.

Louis Chevrolet

CHEVROLET, Louis *(1878–1941)*
Swiss racing driver who arrived in the USA in 1900 to sell a wine pump he had invented. He became a team driver for Buick and, with Etienne Planche, designed the first Chevrolet Six in 1911. He left Chevrolet to found the Frontenac Motor Company, building racing cars and 'go-faster' equipment for Model T Fords.

CHRISTIE, John Walter *(1886–1944)*
Pioneered front-wheel drive in the USA, even competing in the French Grand Prix with huge, if not particularly reliable, fwd racers. He also produced fwd tractor units for fire appliances and built an advanced tank in the 1930s.

CHRYSLER, Walter Percy *(1875–1940)*
A locomotive engineer who joined Buick in 1911, rising to become President – as well as first Vice-President of General Motors. Moved to Willys in 1920, saving this company – and Maxwell-Chalmers – from bankruptcy. He converted Maxwell into the Chrysler Corporation, acquiring Dodge in 1928.

CITROEN, André *(1878–1935)*
Frenchman who worked with Mors pre-World War One, and devised a double chevron gear which was used as the emblem of the car-producing company he founded in 1919. Development of a magnificent new factory and of the classic fwd Citroën car caused his death.

CLEMENT, Adolphe *(1855–1928)*
French cycle manufacturer who made a fortune from the French rights for the Dunlop pneumatic tyre and his exceedingly complex business dealings when he entered the motor car industry. As a result of selling the manufacturing rights to the 'Clément' car, he changed his name to 'Clément-Bayard'. His company also pioneered aeroplanes and airships.

COATALEN, Louis *(1879–1962)*
Breton engineer who came to England in 1900, working for Crowden, Humber and Hillman. His greatest designs were for Sunbeam, where he became Managing Director and built the first V-12 racing car in 1913.

CORD, Erret Lobban *(1894–1974)*
Dynamic entrepreneur who created the Auburn-Duesenberg-Cord empire, and also owned Lycoming engines, American Airlines, Stinson Aircraft and New York Shipbuilding before he was 35.

Gottlieb Daimler

DAIMLER, Gottlieb *(1834–1900)*
Born in Württemberg and trained as an engineer; becoming interested in gas engines in the 1860s, he helped develop the Otto gas engine. During the 1880s he set up on his own to develop a 'universal power source' in the shape of a light petrol engine, in collaboration with Wilhelm Maybach. This engine was fitted into a carriage in 1886, creating the first Daimler car.

DARRACQ, Alexandre *(1855–1931)*
Born in Bordeaux, Darracq entered the cycle industry in 1891, building 'Gladiator' cycles;

selling out in 1896, he moved first into components, then into motor vehicles. Darracq voiturettes were particularly famous. He retired in 1912 to take a financial interest in the Deauville casino. Though Darracq built many thousands of cars, he never drove and disliked riding in them.

Georges Bouton (*left*) and Albert De Dion

DE DION, Albert *(1856–1946)*
Famous as a duellist and gambler, Comte De Dion sponsored two brothers-in-law, Bouton and Trépardoux, in the construction of steam carriages. The first practicable De Dion Bouton petrol engines appeared in 1894 and were fitted to tricycles, voiturettes (for which the marque became renowned) appearing in 1899. De Dion also founded the motoring daily *L'Auto*. He became a Marquis in 1901.

DELAGE, Louis *(1877–1947)*
French builder who supplied components to marques such as Helbe, then made complete Delage light cars from 1906. After 1919, Delage also built luxury cars.

DOBLE, Abner *(1890–1961)*
Built his first steam car in 1906, and drove a prototype to Detroit in 1914 to seek backing. Began production in San Francisco in 1920. Output was always limited, but he gained great acclaim. He later acted as a steam power consultant for overseas firms, including Sentinel steam waggons in England.

DODGE, John *(1864–1920)* **and Horace** *(1868–1920)*
Machinists and cycle makers, the Dodges built transmissions for Olds (1901–02), then made chassis and engines for Henry Ford in return for a tenth of his company. They sold their Ford shares for $25,000,000 and founded the Dodge Brothers company, coining the word 'dependable' to describe their products.

DUESENBERG, Frederick *(1877–1932)*
Designed his first car in 1904, and by 1913 had organized the Duesenberg Motor Company to

build engines. During the 1930s Fred and his brother August built the Duesenberg luxury cars, though E. L. Cord took control of the company in 1927. Fred Duesenberg died in a car crash.

DURANT, William Crapo *(1860–1947)*
Having become a major force in the carriage industry, Billy Durant took over Buick in 1904, then, in 1908, founded the General Motors group. Ousted in 1910, by 1915 he was ready to take over again via his Chevrolet company. However, a share crash in 1920 put him out of GM again, so he established a 'Second Empire' which survived until the Depression.

DURYEA, Charles *(1861–1939)* **and Frank** *(1870–1967)*
In 1893 built the first practicable American car to lead to a production company, the Duryea Motor Power Wagon Company (1896).

EARL, Harley *(1893–1969)*
In the early 1920s was a director of Don Lee Corporation, which built custom coachwork for the wealthy. Became director of 'art and color' at GM in 1927, and is recognized as the first mass-production stylist. Among his styling innovations were tailfins.

S. F. Edge on a 1903 Napier

EDGE, Selwyn Francis *(1868–1940)*
Born in Sydney, New South Wales, came to England and became known as a racing cyclist. Promoted the Napier car and achieving some notable racing victories, including the only British victory in the Gordon Bennett Cup series (1902). In the 1920s, backed AC and Cubitt cars.

FLANDERS, Walter *(1871–1923)*
One of the US car industry's first mass-production experts. He was hired by Ford as production manager in 1908, but left in 1909 to found EMF. Later, he founded the United States Motor Company group.

FORD, Henry *(1863–1947)*
Son of an immigrant Irish farmer, Henry Ford wanted to lift the drudgery off farm life, and became an engineer in Detroit. In 1896 he built his first car. After two unsuccessful attempts to found manufacturing companies, he established the Ford Motor Company on June 16, 1903. He successfully defied the ALAM monopoly group.

FRANKLIN, Herbert *(1867–1956)*
Newspaper proprietor who became a pioneer of die casting, then in 1902 put the first air-cooled Franklin car on the market.

FRAZER, Joseph W. *(1894–1973)*
Having worked for Packard, GM and Pierce-Arrow, Frazer became President of Willys-Overland in 1939 and, with Henry Kaiser, founded Kaiser-Frazer in 1946 in an attempt to break the monopoly of the 'Big Three' in the popular car market.

HAYNES, Elwood G. *(1857–1925)*
Built his first car in 1894 with the help of the Apperson Brothers, and started the Haynes Automobile Company in 1898. He was also a pioneering metallurgist.

ISSIGONIS, Sir Alec *(born 1906)*
Designer of Morris Minor (1948), Mini-Minor (1959) and other fwd British Motor Corporation family cars.

JANO, Vittorio *(1891–1965)*
Italian designer for Fiat, Alfa Romeo and Lancia, for whom he created some of the finest sports and racing cars of all time.

JEFFERY, Thomas B. *(1845–1910)*
An Englishman who emigrated to the USA in 1863, and in 1879 began manufacturing 'Rambler' bicycles. He invented a 'clincher' tyre in 1891, and built his first successful car in 1900. Production of Rambler cars started in 1902.

JOHNSON, Claude *(1864–1926)*
First Secretary of the ACGBI (later the Royal Automobile Club). Introduced Rolls to Royce, and was first Managing Director of Rolls-Royce.

JORDAN, Edward *(1882–1958)*
A journalist who became Advertising Manager of the Thomas B. Jeffery Company, leaving to found the Jordan Motor Car Company in 1916. He became better known for his evocative advertising copy than for his cars.

KELSEY, Cadwallader *(1880–1970)*
Having built an experimental car in 1897, began production of Auto-Tri three-wheelers. Worked for Maxwell as Sales Manager 1905–09, then produced the Motorette car (1910–1912) and the Kelsey car (1921–1924).

KETTERING, Charles F. *(1876–1958)*
'Boss Ket' organized Delco laboratories to develop an electrical ignition system, and subsequently perfected the electric self-starter for the 1911 Cadillac. In 1920 he became head of the GM research laboratories.

KING, Charles Brady *(1868–1957)*
Built Detroit's first motor vehicle in 1896, and later designed the 'Silent Northern' and 'King 8' cars, turning to aeroengines in 1916.

LANCHESTER, Frederick *(1868–1946)*
British pioneer who built an advanced car in 1895. Apart from his contributions to automobile engineering, was one of the great pioneers of aeronautics.

LAWSON, Harry J. *(1852–1925)*
Company promotor, nicknamed 'Father of the British Motor Industry'. Attempted, from 1896, to form a patent monopoly to control the industry, and floated a number of overcapitalized companies, notably Daimler of Coventry (which survived the collapse of his empire in the early 1900s).

LEDWINKA, Hans *(1878–1967)*
Austrian designer who worked for Nesselsdorf, Steyr and Tatra, where he devised backbone chassis, all-independent suspension and air-cooled engines, latterly rear-mounted.

Hans Ledwinka

LORD, Sir Leonard *(1896—1967)*
Chairman of BMC (1952-61), Lord was a brilliant production engineer, who resigned in anger over Morris to join Austin in 1936.. His bitterness created damaging internal rivalries within BMC.

LYONS, Sir William *(1901—1985)*
Founder in 1922 of Swallow Sidecars, which evolved into Jaguar. A brilliantly innovative stylist, he had an unrivalled instinct for designing handsome, keenly-priced cars for sporty drivers.

LELAND, Henry M. *(1843–1932)*
'The Master of Precision' learned his art in the arms industry. He also invented the mechanical hair-clipper and began building engines. He reorganized the Henry Ford Company as Cadillac after Ford resigned in 1902, later founding Lincoln.

LENOIR, J.-J. Etienne *(1822–1900)*
A Belgian, he invented a successful method of enamelling clock faces in 1847, and in the late 1850s devised a gas engine. He built his first horseless carriage in Paris in 1862, later selling it to the Czar of Russia.

LEVASSOR, Emile *(1844–1897)*
Co-founder of Panhard-Levassor and inventor of the *Système Panhard*, in which the engine was at the front, under a bonnet, driving the rear wheels via a sliding-pinion gearbox. Died as a delayed effect of a racing accident.

MARKUS, Seigfried *(1831–1898)*
Austrian inventor who built a number of experimental internal combustion-engined test-benches from 1868. His first true car, long claimed to have been built in 1875, is now known to date from the late 1880s.

MAXWELL, Jonathan Dixon *(1864–1968)*
Starting in the cycle industry with Elmer Apperson, he worked on the 1894 Haynes-Apperson. In 1903, he joined Ben Briscoe to found the Maxwell-Briscoe company.

METZ, Charles *(1864–1937)*
Famed for his Orient cycles, Metz began production of the crude Orient Buckboard. In 1909 he introduced the low-priced friction-drive Metz 22, sold initially for home assembly.

MORRIS, William *(1877–1963)*
Starting as an Oxford cycle agent, Morris (who became Lord Nuffield) built his first Morris-Oxford light car in 1912, and came to dominate the British motor industry in the 1920s. He was renowned for his philanthropy.

NASH, Charles W. *(1864–1948)*
An itinerant farm worker, Charles Nash joined the Durant-Dort carriage company, then moved to Buick with Billy Durant, becoming President of that company in 1910 and of the whole GM group in 1912. He left to take over Jeffery and transform it into the Nash Motor Company.

OLDS, Ransom Eli *(1864–1950)*
Claimed to have built his first steam car in 1896, and his first petrol car in 1894. Success came with the 1901 Curved-Dash Oldsmobile. He later founded Reo, and also invented an early motor mower.

PENNINGTON, Edmund Joel *(1858–1911)*
American 'mechanical charlatan', who 'invented' an airship in 1885, and produced a number of eccentric motor vehicles which defied normal mechanical laws.

PEUGEOT, Armand *(1849–1915)*
Son of one of France's leading ironmongers, Peugeot translated his firm's expertise in making steel rods to replace whalebone in crinoline skirts into the manufacture of cycles. In 1889 the Peugeot company built a steam car designed by Serpollet, but then constructed tubular-framed Daimler-engined cars, France's first production cars.

POPE, Albert Augustus *(1843–1909)*
Colonel Pope founded a successful cycle manufacturing group in 1879, and moved into the motor industry via electric vehicles as early as 1896. Pope's motor group was dragged down by the decline of the cycle business.

PORSCHE, Ferdinand *(1875–1952)*
Austrian designer for Steyr, Austro-Daimler, Mercedes, Auto-Union, Cisitalia and Porsche, he created the original Volkswagen in the 1930s.

Ferdinand Porsche

PORTER, Finley Robertson *(1872–1964)*
Designed the classic Mercer Raceabout, as well as FRP and Porter cars, becoming Chief Engineer of Curtiss Aircraft in 1919.

RENAULT, Louis *(1877–1944)*
Son of a rich Parisian button maker, Louis Renault rebuilt his De Dion tricycle into a shaft-driven voiturette in 1898, and received so many orders that he began production of similar vehicles. By 1900, Renault was building 350 cars a year and was established as one of France's leading makes. Louis Renault died in prison during World War Two, having been accused of collaborating with the Germans during the Occupation of France.

RIKER, Andrew L. *(1868–1930)*
Built his first electric tricycle in 1884, but did not begin production until 1899. In 1902 joined Locomobile to design their first petrol cars.

ROESCH, Georges *(1891–1969)*
Brilliant Swiss engineer who became Chief Engineer of Clement Talbot of London at 25, designing high speed tourers of great refinement.

ROLLS, The Hon. Charles Stuart
(1877–1910)
Interested in machinery from an early age, Lord Llangottock's youngest son was a pioneer motorist and racing driver who entered the motor trade. Anxious to sell a car bearing his own name, he joined with the engineer Royce. Rolls died in a flying accident at Bournemouth, having been the first man to fly the English Channel both ways.

The Hon. C. S. Rolls (*left*) and Henry Royce

ROYCE, Henry *(1863–1933)*
Electrical engineer who built a twin-cylinder car in 1903, and went on to construct the 'best car in the world' as well as some remarkable aeroengines.

SELDEN, George Baldwin *(1846–1932)*
A patent attorney who experimented with engines from 1873 to 1875, and designed a self-propelled vehicle on which he filed a patent in 1879, the patent being granted in 1895. He sold the patent to Columbia Electric on a royalty basis in 1899, when it was used to try and create a monopoly group (Association of Licenced Automobile Manufacturers).

SERPOLLET, Léon *(1858–1907)*
Frenchman who devised the flash boiler for rapid production of steam, and built a steam tricycle in 1887. He built a number of steam three-wheelers in the 1890s, but did not seriously begin car production until the turn of the century. His sprint racers broke many speed records. His aim was to build a steamer that was as simple to control as a petrol vehicle, but his death from consumption ended the Serpollet company.

Frederick Simms

SIMMS, Frederick R. *(1863–1944)*
Brought the first Daimler engines into Britain in 1891, and fitted these power units into motor launches on the Thames. Formed the Daimler Motor Syndicate in 1893, which was taken over by Lawson interests in 1896. He invented the name 'motor-car', and helped to found the Automobile Club of Great Britain and Ireland (later the Royal Automobile Club) and the Society of Motor Manufacturers and Traders. He also built Simms cars.

SLOAN, Alfred P. *(1875–1966)*
At Durant's behest, formed the United Motors Corporation of accessory manufacturers, which was later absorbed by GM. An administrative genius, Sloan reorganized the corporate structure of GM, becoming its President from 1923–1936.

STANLEY, Francis E. *(1849–1918)* **and Freelan O.** *(1849–1940)*
The Stanley twins used the proceeds from the sale of their photographic dry-plate business to develop a steam car, the rights to which were bought for $250,000 to create Locomobile. The Stanleys came up with an improved design, Stanley steamers being built into the 1920s.

STUTZ, Harry *(1871–1930)*
Designed an improved rear axle, then became Sales Manager for Schebler carburettors, engineer for Marion and designer of the American Underslung. Manufacture of Stutz cars began in 1911; Harry Stutz resigned in 1919, later founding HCS. He was also a talented saxophonist.

THOMAS, Edwin Ross *(1850–1936)*
Though he founded the E. R. Thomas Motor Company in Buffalo, NY, in 1900 (it built the Thomas Flyer which won the round-the-world New York-Paris Race of 1908), Edwin Thomas never learned to drive.

VOISIN, Gabriel *(1880–1973)*
French aviation pioneer who went into car production between the wars with advanced and unorthodox sleeve-valve cars.

WHITE, Windsor *(1866–1958)*, **Rollin** *(1872–1968)* **and Walter** *(1876–1929)*
Rollin and Windsor built the first White Steamer in 1900, and Walter was sent to London the next year to develop the European market. Rollin left the White Company (Windsor was its President) in 1914 to build Cleveland tractors, and launched the Rollin car in 1923.

WILLS, Childe Harold *(1878–1940)*
A brilliant metallurgist who helped Henry Ford develop his first cars (and also designed the famous 'Ford' script logo) and became Chief Engineer of the Ford Motor Company. He developed vanadium and molybdenum steel alloys for the motor industry. With his severance pay from Ford he founded Wills Ste Claire. In 1933 he became Chrysler's chief metallurgist.

Childe Harold Wills

WILLYS, John North *(1873–1933)*
In 1906 undertook to sell the entire output of Overland, then mounted an effort to save the company when it got into difficulties in 1907, moving production to Toledo. He built Overland production up to 95,000 units – second only to Ford – in 1915.

WINTON, Alexander *(1860–1932)*
Scots marine engineer who jumped ship in America in 1880, starting bicycle production in 1896. Built his first car in 1896, founding the Winton Motor Carriage Company next year. In 1903, he launched an eight-cylinder 'Bullet' racer. His designs featured pneumatic controls. When car production was suspended in 1924, he began manufacture of diesel engines.